Fight or Flight No More: The S

Tristen Paradis

Special thanks to Consor Joy Bulaquena for the wonderful cover artwork

Disclaimer: Consult with your health care professional first and foremost. Do not change doses or go off of medication without consulting your doctor.

Nothing would make me happier than knowing that I helped even one person to overcome their anxiety

Table of Contents

Introduction

The solution to anxiety, that's what this book is about. That's also why this book is so short. I didn't want to get distracted by any fluff.

I know how painful anxiety is; it's one definition of hell. Getting you the information that saved me, and continues to save me, is of utmost importance. I cannot guarantee that the solution that worked for me will work for you, but in my opinion, if it worked for me it will work for you. Why do I think that? Because we are both *homo sapiens*.

The only reason I have waited so long to write this book was because I wanted to be sure that my anxiety disorder was gone for good. It's been two years since I've had an anxiety attack. This is proof enough for me that the solution I used wasn't just a fluke.

There are so many people out there who suffer from anxiety without knowing what to do. An acquaintance of mine recently posted a status update on Facebook, pleading for answers from anyone about anxiety cures; the answers that people gave in the comments were all variations of "Smoke some weed."

That brings me to the title of this book. I say that I have found *the* anxiety solution, but there are other ways that people deal with anxiety. Medical marijuana is a common way, and so are benzodiazepines. The difference is, these ways of dealing are only bandage solutions, and not even good bandage solutions. They require you to live under a different state of mind than is natural for you. And they require your allegiance to them for the rest of your life.

The solution that is the focus of this book is meditation. Meditation does not require you to be religious and it does not require you to hum. It does not require you to be spiritual. There are different paths that you may choose to go down if you want to further your meditation practice, but for the purposes of curing anxiety, it is completely health based.

My Story

The following is not my life story, so don't worry. It is just a brief recount of my experience living in the hell of anxiety. You may be able to relate to some of it. If however, you want to skip ahead to the solution section, my feelings will not be hurt.

A friend once told me that an anxiety attack was like being trapped inside a large grandfather clock and the time was wrong. I don't believe this would make any sense to someone who has never experienced an attack, but it made a lot of sense to me.

In my first year of University, I had aspirations to become a medical doctor. I knew it would be a hard road, but I felt ready to take on the world.

A few months into school, I discovered just how hard it would be. I was consistently achieving mediocre grades. The stress was piling on.

At the same time I met a girl in my program. We quickly became friends. Friends quickly became not enough for me. I wanted more. I asked her out and she declined.

Looking back, I wish I had stopped hanging out with her after that point, but instead we hung out every day, and I became even more infatuated with her.

At the start of the second semester, the weight of my mediocre grades and my feelings of infatuation for my friend hit a breaking point. I would never be a doctor and I would never be with her.

I don't know exactly what the threshold is for someone to trigger an anxiety disorder. I don't think there is a standard. It could be situations much heavier than mine, or lighter. And it could be that a lot of people just grew up with lots of anxiety. I'm sure that was even my case to some degree. These memories just stood out as the breaking point in my mind.

I remember saying goodbye to that girl one day, and as I walked away, my vision got kind of blurry. My body surged with energy and I felt the need to escape to somewhere. But I didn't know where. I got the thought, "Maybe I need to use the bathroom." I felt like I needed to pee. I speed walked into the nearest building and into the nearest bathroom. Upon using the bathroom I felt better.

After that incident, which I soon realized was an anxiety attack, I equated that feeling with needing to use the bathroom. I couldn't be in a closed room or in a situation where it would be frowned upon to leave to the bathroom, at least not for very long. This was very difficult as I was a University student. I was always stuck in 50 minute classes. I had a very hard time sitting through these, and I never remembered the last 20 minutes or so because the anxiety had already set in so strong.

I have one memory in particular of sitting in class and feeling the anxiety. I suddenly felt like I had to leave the classroom, because the world was ending in there. I quickly shoved my books into my bag and stood up abruptly. I ran up the stairs of the lecture hall and escaped through the door. Outside I still felt the adrenaline pumping. It still felt like something terrible was happening. I looked around and everyone outside was talking, or laughing, or studying. No one else felt this certain doom. Why did I?

Over the next couple of months I had frequent anxiety attacks at school. On a good day I would have one. On a bad day I would have more.

Coming home from school, I would feel exhausted. I just wanted to lay in bed.

I became afraid of leaving my house. Just the walk outside to my car was daunting. Feeling the anxiety as I got into my car, I would laugh at how ridiculous my life had become.

The semester finished and a weight was lifted. I spent the next month at home, mostly watching TV. I didn't know it at the time, but I was severely depressed.

My summer job landscaping started and I somehow managed to survive being out in the city parks for two hour intervals at a time.

I still felt the anxiety, and sometimes I would have attacks, but I was faring better than I had at school.

Even though I was doing better, I still called in sick once a week. Thankfully it was a government job, so they were very lenient about that sort of thing.

Even though I was doing better, I still had daily thoughts of suicide.

I had once been very social. I would go to parties all the time. But that was no more. The anxiety forced me to change my lifestyle. And I hated this new lifestyle.

I remember one night I was going to try clubbing with some friends. We pre-drank at my one buddy's house. A couple drinks in I felt the anxiety of going all the way downtown. I had an attack. When it was time for everyone to leave, I told my friends I didn't feel good. I stayed at my buddy's house and watched TV while they all went out to have fun.

At the start of my second year, the attacks returned as they were before, every day. There was no way I could keep living like this. I went to a doctor.

The doctor prescribed me a fairly high dose of Wellbutrin XL. It was technically an anti-depressant, but it worked differently than most. It gave a stimulant effect somewhat related to speed.

The drug cleared my thoughts. It helped me out of the deep depression I was in.

I now remember a counsellor telling me about meditation, but it was suggested so offhandedly that I forgot about it at the time. I truly wish someone had ordered me to try the practice of meditation, because it took me a couple more months of suffering before I found it.

I came across mindfulness meditation as a cure for anxiety and decided to follow along with directions on a website.

It was so simple and yet so profound.

Within a week or so, I already noticed a decrease in anxiety. And I had practiced this meditation on only a few days that week. This sparked my interest in mindfulness meditation, and so I researched the hell out of it.

As soon as I practiced meditation every day of the week, I stopped having anxiety attacks completely.

The question you might have is, what role did the Wellbutrin have to play in this?

Soon after the attacks stopped, I went down to the lowest dose. I initially feared that it was the combination of the drug and meditation that was keeping my anxiety levels down. My fears were unfounded. I actually felt *less* anxiety at the lowest dose.

A month later I decided to cut the drug completely. I haven't had an anxiety attack since. Nor have I been depressed.

For the majority of people out there, going on a drug such as Wellbutrin XL is not necessary. I only went on it because of depression. And now I wonder if I had found meditation sooner, if the drug would have been necessary at all.

Of course if you are taking medication for anxiety or depression, don't just go off of it without consulting with your doctor first.

These days life is good. I've come back to the place I was before the major anxiety disorder was triggered. I've picked up the pieces so to speak.

Now, when I leave the house and I walk to my car, I hold my head up high. I smile with confidence. The world is no longer hostile or chaotic; it just is what it is.

The path I've decided to walk on is different from the one I had set upon five years ago when I started University. That's right, I'm now graduated with a Bachelor of Science in Environmental Science. Not quite a doctor, but hey, I likely didn't have the aptitude required to become one. And if I did have the aptitude, I couldn't handle the stress. There's no shame in changing your situation if it becomes too stressful.

Now that summer is over, I've just finished at my landscaping job. I had a wonderful season free from anxiety and depression. And now, I'm looking forward to starting a career job with an environmental company. Of course I'm nervous, but it's a healthy nervous-excitement!

As far as dating is concerned, I've come along way from being infatuated with my friend from years back. It took about two years until I felt confident and stable enough to start dating again, but in the last few months I've gone on a couple of dates. They haven't become anything serious, but that's okay! I feel like now I should have some fun, seeing as I have a few years to make up for.

Relationships of the romantic persuasion are really going to depend on who you are. You could get back on that horse a couple of months after you start your meditation practice. Or maybe you're still managing to make things work despite your anxiety. Either way, I bet your romantic life will benefit.

An increase in self-esteem has been a major result of overcoming the anxiety disorder. It's definitely factored into me writing this book. It's amazing what an increase in self esteem can do for your life!

Anxiety and Drinking

As a heavy drinker, I have always been susceptible to alcohol induced anxiety. I know many others who suffer from it after every weekend that they drink.

On days that I am hungover, I will admit that it is hard to practice meditation. It's just hard to focus. However, I do practice anyway, even if I can only muster the strength while lying in bed.

Since practicing meditation consistently, I have never been overwhelmed by alcohol induced anxiety. The most I experience are feelings of shame or embarrassment from thoughts of what I may or may not have done the night before. But I am always able to let these thoughts go. I no longer dwell on them. I let them go and instead I cherish all of the good memories.

Anxiety and Caffeine

I have heard from a number of people that caffeine seemed to trigger their anxiety attacks. Looking back now, my overdependence on caffeine was likely a contributing factor to my development of the anxiety disorder.

If you're a caffeine junkie and you experience more than normal levels of anxiety, it may be a good idea to tone it down a bit.

Once I realized that I had an anxiety disorder, I cut caffeine out completely. Mind you, it was mostly because I no longer needed it. I remember joking to my dad that a silver lining to having anxiety was that I no longer had to spend money on coffee or energy drinks. My body was always running on overdrive anyways. There was no danger of me falling asleep in class.

Now that I've overcome the anxiety disorder, I have cautiously reintroduced caffeine into my life. I have a cup of green tea nearly every day. It helps me to get over that sleepy time right after lunch, when I feel like I'm going to slip into a food coma.

The Solution

Mindfulness meditation is one of the many different meditations in the Buddhist arsenal and was brought into the western medical world by Dr. Jon Kabat-Zinn.

The central idea behind mindfulness meditation is being awake in the present moment. It is meant to take a person out of delusional thoughts and to reconnect that person to reality. That is why it is the perfect solution for people suffering from anxiety. Anxiety is a product of delusional thoughts. Once a person can see these thoughts for what they are, the anxiety will break away.

The Simple Meditation

First, place one or two pillows onto the floor. Set an alarm for ten minutes. Sit your butt on the pillows and cross your legs, resting them on the ground. Rest your hands on your knees.

Close your eyes or keep them open. If you close them, then just stare at the black abyss that is your eyclids. If they are open, then stare at anything.

Concentrate on your breathing. Focus on the feeling of the in breath, the out breath, and the resting period. This is the natural breathing rhythm of your body. Do not exert any effort to change this rhythm. Just keep your focus on the feeling of the breath for every cycle.

If you realize that you have lost your concentration on the breath, then simply refocus your concentration on the breath, every time this happens. The more and more you practice, the better your concentration will become.

Once the alarm rings or buzzes, the meditation session is complete.

This is a simple meditation, but it can be very powerful with consistent practice.

The Spider Exercise

Before I come to a slightly more complicated meditation, I will explain an exercise that helped me understand what was fueling my anxiety.

Just as before, place one or two pillows onto the floor. Set an alarm for ten minutes. Sit your butt on these and cross your legs, resting them on the ground. Rest your hands on your knees.

For this exercise your eyes must be closed.

Concentrate on your breathing, just as you did in the simple meditation. Focus on the feeling of the in breath, the out breath, and the resting period.

Hopefully you can feel a sensation on your body somewhere, an itch or a tingle. If you cannot feel any annoyance on your body for the entire ten minutes, then that's okay. You just did the simple meditation.

If you are able to feel an annoying sensation somewhere, then focus your attention on it, while also keeping focus on your breathing cycle. Imagine that this itch or tingle is a spider, or a centipede, or something that really disgusts you. Don't imagine a spider if you have arachnophobia, you don't want to be terrified. Imagine that it is biting into your skin with it's little fangs or pincers. Keep focusing on this. Keep your eyes closed.

When and only when the alarm goes off can you open your eyes and check that spot to be sure that there isn't actually a spider there. And that's just the point. It may be difficult to hold out that long, but by doing so, you are training yourself to not blindly trust your thoughts and feelings.

Thoughts are very often wrong, and yet our first instincts are to trust them. There was no spider there in actuality, but I bet after a few minutes passed, it felt like there really was. Our thoughts are convincing, even if we know they are fake! And we knew the spider was fake, because we created it.

The fake spider likely caused you to feel anxiety. The anxiety level felt may have been low, or it may have been very high. Other thoughts that trigger feelings of anxiety are not so obvious because we do not make a conscious effort to create them like we did with the fake spider. Mindfulness meditation practice enables us to identify these thoughts that cause our anxious feelings, and by identifying them, they lose their power over us.

The Mind

In the context of mindfulness meditation, it is not a perfect analogy, but still very useful to say that the mind is another one of our senses.

Like our hearing, which allows us to detect sounds, our mind allows us to detect thoughts. Sounds are made up of sound waves, and thoughts are made up of electrical impulses from the brain. And just like we can choose our response to an obnoxious sound, we can choose our response to an obnoxious thought.

Thoughts are not what make people who they are. The sounds that people hear do not define the people themselves, and neither do thoughts in the mind. It is important to realize that we are not our anxious thoughts, and they are not a part of us.

Out of all of the senses humans have, the mind is the strongest. Sure, we enjoy music that we hear, and the smell of roses, but we are the most attached to thoughts.

Thoughts are frequently out of touch with reality, and anxious thoughts are always. So, it is important to let go of our attachment to thoughts.

Of course, we are able to use thoughts productively. Not all of them are detrimental to our wellbeing. But, we must have the ability to choose which thoughts we will give our energy to, and which thoughts we will let go of. Mindfulness meditation nurtures this ability.

The Expanded Meditation

Place one or two pillows on the floor. Set an alarm for fifteen minutes. Sit your butt on the pillows and then cross your legs, resting them on the ground. Rest the top of each hand on each knee.

Focus your eyes on a specific spot. It can be anything, the leg of a chair, the radiator, the closet door, wherever. The point is that you *see* what you are looking at.

Now listen to the sounds around you. The dog may be barking, or a neighbor might be yelling next door, or there might just be the buzzing of silence. Either way, it is important that you *hear*.

Remaining focused on your sight and hearing, now you will also *feel*. Pay attention to the feeling of your butt on the pillows, your legs on the ground, your hands against your knees, and even the itch on your neck.

We are not used to focusing in on many senses at once, so this may be a really interesting experience.

Notice now that your body is breathing. Focus on the breathing as well; the in breath and the out breath, and the resting period. Pay attention to every second of each phase of breathing. Focus on your body's breathing intently.

You will now experience all of the above senses, coupled with the feeling of your breathing cycle.

With some practice, instead of becoming immediately attached to thoughts that pop up in your mind, you will see them for what they are, thoughts. They too can be held in your focus.

The difference between holding thoughts in your focus and becoming attached to them is that when you attach to thoughts, you lose focus of everything else. By holding thoughts in your focus, they are treated as being no different than hearing the dog barking, or feeling your legs cramping. They are just here, in this moment.

Once the alarm rings or buzzes, the meditation session is over.

The Goal in Meditation

I find that I get more out of a meditation session if I have a goal in mind going in.

The best goal to have in your mind when getting over anxiety is to become fully awake to your life, as much as possible. A person might equate overwhelming anxiety to being trapped inside a waking nightmare, but you can only experience this nightmare if you are "asleep." As you practice more and more you will fully understand what this means.

Time Investment

The time investment required with practicing mindfulness meditation is small considering how life changing it can be. Plus, a side benefit of meditation is that the days are functionally longer. Being fully awake to more moments means that you experience more of your day, and in turn you become more productive.

At first it may be difficult to sit for any time longer than ten minutes. That's okay. Try to do at least ten minutes.

Optimally, for the sake of overcoming anxiety, you will want to sit down and practice for 15 – 20 minutes a day.

From my experience, 15 minutes of meditation is more beneficial than sleeping in for 15 more minutes. Yes, I believe that meditation in the morning is the best time.

If you cannot find time to practice in the morning, then the afternoon is fine too. At night before bed seems to be nice because it's easier to fall asleep, but it really doesn't help for the next day. If you enjoy practicing at night, then try practicing in the morning too. I usually do 15 minutes in the morning and five minutes at night.

If on a particular day you are running late and won't have any time for yourself later on, then sitting down for five minutes will suffice. The shortest time span I've sat down to practice for was two minutes, and even that was a benefit.

As you get further into practicing, you may feel the desire to sit for longer periods of time. That is fine.

In everyday life, you will be able to connect with your senses more easily. Connecting with your senses will wake you up to the moment. The most valuable sense for this purpose is feeling, in particular, the feeling of your breathing cycle. At least it is for me. It may be the sense of sound for you. Or you may be able to connect with all of the senses you normally do when practicing the expanded meditation. Focus on what you find is most effective in waking you up to the present moment.

This does not mean that you stop driving, or stop writing your test. You continue whatever activity you were doing, but now, you are connected with your senses and the present moment. It is also important to note that the point of reconnecting with your senses is solely to wake you up to the moment, not really to experience the stimuli that the senses are bringing you.

It is especially important to focus on your sense(s) when you have anxious thoughts. Doing so will distance you from the thoughts, and allow you to choose whether you want to attach to these thoughts, or let them go.

Doing the above may not be so easy at first. If it isn't, don't let that stress you out. It will come with daily practice.

The meditations I have in this book are guidelines.

Do whatever enables you to connect with the present moment. For example, you may decide to focus on the feeling of the breath coming in and out of your nostrils. You may want to focus on fewer senses at a time, or maybe even more. It's really up to you.

If you are unable to sit on pillows on the ground cross legged, then sit on a chair. Or you can lay on a mat on the ground. Typically laying in bed is not a good idea. That's where you fall asleep, not where you wake up.

Anyone who needs further guidance can feel free to email me at tristenparadis@hotmail.com. Below is a list of frequently asked questions.

FAQs

How often should I do the spider exercise?

Not very often. I've only done it about five or six times in the last two years. It's really just to show people how powerful anxious thoughts can be.

Is the simple meditation better or the expanded meditation?

They are both equally useful if they wake you up to the present moment. I really just ordered each meditation chronologically, from the first one I practiced, to the one I am currently practicing. I developed the spider exercise by accident while practicing the simple meditation.

I keep getting bored when I'm sitting there. Am I doing something wrong?

No, not at all. Any feelings that you experience are natural and are part of the present moment. When you feel boredom, just include this feeling in your focus. It is simply a part of your practice session.

Just sitting in one spot for an extended length of time is giving me anxiety. How do I get over this?

You will want to focus in on the feeling of anxiety itself. It is just a feeling. That is all. The reason that you start to feel anxiety is that your mind has become attached to anxious thoughts. Try to become aware of the anxious thoughts that are fueling this feeling. Once you see these thoughts for what they are, they should dissipate.

These anxious thoughts and feelings are just another part of the practice session.

Science and Meditation

As a science student, I couldn't help but include a small blurb on science and meditation.

There is a lot of evidence out there supporting the idea that if a person does proper brain exercises, the neurological systems in the brain can be modified in structure (1). This means that the gray matter of certain areas can be physically increased in concentration (1). And of course, each area of the brain is in charge of different faculties (1). I think you can see where this is going.

A study was done by Holzel et al. (1) to determine the effect of mindfulness meditation on the brain. They wanted to see if meditation would cause changes in gray matter concentrations (1). First of all, in case you're wondering, no areas of the brain experienced decreases in gray matter (1). Their results showed an increase in gray matter concentrations for areas in charge of stress response, emotion regulation, perception of self, and the experience of spatial unity of the self and body (1). These are all factors that would improve a person's ability to deal with anxious thoughts and feelings!

The take away from this study is that meditation physically changes your brain, improving your ability to live in the moment, and therefore deal with anxiety. If you need a long term goal to keep you motivated in your daily practice, this could be it.

Additional Resources

What I have included in this book was information based on everything I required to cure my anxiety disorder. There are further benefits to maintaining a daily meditation practice. If you are interested in delving deeper, these two books are great resources:

"Where ever you go there you are," By Jon Kabat-Zinn and "Full Catastrophe Living," Also by Jon Kabat-Zinn.

If you google mindfulness meditation plus where you live, you should be able to find local groups or classes that you can attend if you desire. Personally, I don't feel the need to practice in the presence of other people, but many people do enjoy it, so it's up to you.

A Note on Transcendental Meditation

If you research meditation at any length, you are sure to come across Transcendental Meditation. It is a movement that has been going on for many years, but recently it has picked up steam as some notable celebrities have gotten involved. To become a member of this movement, the fee is quite large (at least $1000 USD). With that, you receive an instructor and they teach you a specialized meditation technique during a number of in-person sessions. If you're rolling in money, this might be an interesting experience, otherwise I would advise against it.

The entire internet is quite secretive on what exactly the Transcendental Meditation technique involves. However, from what I can gather, it is simply mantra meditation.

From what I have read, mantra meditation has many of the same benefits as mindfulness meditation. Although I cannot back that up from personal experience.

Nevertheless, if you are interested in mantra meditation, I have read a great book on the topic:

"Deep Meditation: Pathway to Personal Freedom," By Yogani.

1. Hölzel, B.K., Carmody, J., Vangel, M., Congleton, C., Yerramsetti, S.M., Gard, T., & S.W., Lazar. (2011). Mindfulness practice leads to increases in regional brain gray matter density. *Psychiatric research: Neuroimaging* **36 – 43.**

I would greatly appreciate if you gave me a review on Amazon, as this will increase the visibility of this book to others.

I thank you for reading, and I wish you the best on your journey to overcoming anxiety!

Printed in Great Britain
by Amazon